On Christian Liberty

FACETS

Selected Titles in the Facets Series

On Christian Liberty

Martin Luther

Translated by W. A. Lambert
Revised by Harold J. Grimm

Fortress Press
Minneapolis

ON CHRISTIAN LIBERTY

This work is excerpted from volume 31 of *Luther's Works,* edited by Harold J. Grimm and Helmut T. Lehmann, © 1957 Fortress Press.

Introduced by Roy A. Harrisville, III

Cover image: Castle church in Wittenberg
Cover and book design: Joseph P. Bonyata

ISBN: 0-8006-3607-4

Contents

Introduction

Martin Luther stands as one of the most significant figures in Western history. His distinction as the father of the Protestant Reformation is augmented by his innovative use of new technology (the printing press), his translation of the Christian Bible into the vernacular, and his impact upon European society. Indeed, his legacy continues to this day in the Lutheran denominations around the world and the respect his theological formulations enjoy in the whole Christian church.

Born in 1483 to middle-class parents in the area of Saxony in eastern Germany, he became an Augustinian monk, a priest, a professor of biblical literature, a reformer, a husband and father. He died in 1546 after having witnessed the birth of a renewal movement that would result in a profound shift in faith, politics, and society. Not all results would prove beneficial, and much suffering would come from those who opposed and those who supported his ideas. Not until the end of the Thirty Years War in the next century would his followers and his enemies lay down their arms.

He has been praised and vilified for what he began and preached and wrote. Some of it must be judged by the context of his day, some of it must be criticized by the lights of his own beliefs, and some of it shines with the luster of divine reflection. However his work is judged, it cannot be avoided, for his impact upon church and society endures in the faith and hope of millions.

Martin Luther's treatise, or written argument, *On Christian Liberty* (*The Freedom of a Christian*), remains one of the most influential of his many works. In 1517 an obscure professor in the town of Wittenberg issued a list of Ninety-five

Theses, or propositions, that called for repentance, an end to the sale of indulgences (expensive pieces of paper that assured them or a deceased relative of relief from punishment after death for sin), and a church council to debate such matters. By 1520 Luther's views had been published widely in such treatises as *The Address to the German Nobility* and *On the Babylonian Captivity of the Church*, both written in that year and both attacking certain aspects of the church, including the papal see (the seat of a bishop's office or authority). He had appeared in two meetings, one in Augsburg (1518) and the other at Leipzig (1519) to defend his views.

Now on September 6, 1520, Luther had been persuaded to write *On Christian Liberty* at the request of his mentor and head of his monastic order in Germany, Johann von Staupitz, and his successor, Wenceslaus Link. Both men had been prevailed upon by the pope's emissary, Karl von Miltitz, to urge Luther to write a conciliatory letter to Pope Leo X in a final effort to prevent a split in the church and assure the Pope that Luther had not attacked him personally. Miltitz met with Luther himself on October 12 to press the case. By this time, however, the Pope had issued an ultimatum on June 15 that if Luther did not renounce his views within sixty days, he and all his followers would be excommunicated from the church.

Luther agreed to write the letter to Pope Leo (included at the end of this book) and also a devotional book to accompany it. Both were penned in Latin, as was customary in the church of those days. If the Pope ever read the letter or the treatise, he would have found in the treatise a succinct and clear expression of Luther's evangelical theology. The Christian, Luther declared, is perfectly free from sin, death, and the devil through faith in Christ. At the same time, this does not give license to the Christian to act as he or she wishes, but rather bestows on believers the marvelous opportunity to serve their neighbors. For that is what God, in Christ, has done for his children.

Martin Luther's Treatise

On Christian Liberty
[The Freedom of a Christian]

Many people have considered Christian faith an easy thing, and not a few have given it a place among the virtues. They do this because they have not experienced it and have never tasted the great strength there is in faith. It is impossible to write well about it or to understand what has been written about it unless one has at one time or another experienced the courage which faith gives a man when trials oppress him. But he who has had even a faint taste of it can never write, speak, meditate, or hear enough concerning it. It is a living "spring of water welling up to eternal life," as Christ calls it in John 4[:14].

As for me, although I have no wealth of faith to boast of and know how scant my supply is, I nevertheless hope that I have attained to a little faith, even though I have been assailed by great and various temptations; and I hope that I can discuss it, if not more elegantly, certainly more to the point, than those literalists and subtle disputants have previously done, who have not even understood what they have written.

To make the way smoother for the unlearned—for only them do I serve—I shall set down the following two propositions concerning the freedom and the bondage of the spirit:

A Christian is a perfectly free lord of all, subject to none.

A Christian is a perfectly dutiful servant of all, subject to all.

These two theses seem to contradict each other. If, however, they should be found to fit together they would serve our purpose beautifully. Both are Paul's own statements, who says in 1 Cor. 9[:19],

"For though I am free from all men, I have made myself a slave to all," and in Rom. 13[:8], "Owe no one anything, except to love one another." Love by its very nature is ready to serve and be subject to him who is loved. So Christ, although he was Lord of all, was "born of woman, born under the law" [Gal. 4:4], and therefore was at the same time a free man and a servant, "in the form of God" and "of a servant" [Phil. 2:6–7].

Let us start, however, with something more remote from our subject, but more obvious. Man has a twofold nature, a spiritual and a bodily one. According to the spiritual nature, which men refer to as the soul, he is called a spiritual, inner, or new man. According to the bodily nature, which men refer to as flesh, he is called a carnal, outward, or old man, of whom the Apostle writes in 2 Cor. 4[:16], "Though our outer nature is wasting away, our inner nature is being renewed every day." Because of this diversity of nature the Scriptures assert contradictory things concerning the same man, since these two men in the same man contradict each other, "for the desires of the flesh are against the Spirit, and the desires of the Spirit are against the flesh," according to Gal. 5[:17].

First, let us consider the inner man to see how a righteous, free, and pious Christian, that is, a spiritual, new, and inner man, becomes what he is. It is evident that no external thing has any influence in producing Christian righteousness or freedom, or in producing unrighteousness or servitude. A simple argument will furnish the proof of this statement. What can it profit the soul if the body is well, free, and active, and eats, drinks, and does as it pleases? For in these respects even the most godless slaves of vice may prosper. On the other hand, how will poor health or imprisonment or hunger or thirst or any other external misfortune harm the soul? Even the most godly men, and those who are free because of clear consciences, are afflicted with these things. None of these things touch either the freedom or the servitude of the soul. It does not help the soul if the body is adorned with the sacred robes of priests or dwells in sacred places or is occupied with sacred duties or prays, fasts, abstains from certain kinds of food, or does any work that can be done by the body and in the body. The righteousness and the freedom of the soul require something far different since the things which have been mentioned could be done by any wicked person. Such works produce nothing but hypocrites. On the other hand, it will not harm the soul if the body is clothed in secular dress, dwells in unconsecrated places, eats and drinks as others do, does not pray aloud, and neglects to do all the above-mentioned things which hypocrites can do.

Furthermore, to put aside all kinds of works, even contemplation, meditation, and all that the soul can do, does not help. One thing, and only one thing, is necessary for Christian life, righteousness, and freedom. That one thing is the most holy Word of God, the gospel of Christ, as Christ says, John 11[:25], "I am the resurrection and the life; he who believes in me, though he die, yet shall he live"; and John 8[:36], "So if the Son makes you free, you will be free indeed"; and Matt. 4[:4], "Man shall not live by bread alone, but by every word that proceeds from the mouth of God." Let us then consider it certain and firmly established that the soul can do without anything except the Word of God and that where the Word of God is missing there is no help at all for the soul. If it has the Word of God it is rich and lacks nothing since it is the Word of life, truth, light, peace, righteousness, salvation, joy, liberty, wisdom, power, grace, glory, and of every incalculable blessing. This is why the prophet in the entire Psalm [119] and in many other places yearns and sighs for the Word of God and uses so many names to describe it.

On the other hand, there is no more terrible disaster with which the wrath of God can afflict men than a famine of the hearing of his Word, as he says in Amos [8:11]. Likewise there is no greater mercy than when he sends forth his Word, as we read in Psalm 107[:20]: "He sent forth his word, and healed them, and delivered them from destruction." Nor was Christ sent into the world for any other ministry except that of the Word. Moreover, the entire spiritual estate—all the apostles, bishops, and priests—has been called and instituted only for the ministry of the Word.

You may ask, "What then is the Word of God, and how shall it be used, since there are so many words of God?" I answer: The Apostle explains this in Romans 1. The Word is the gospel of God concerning his Son, who was made flesh, suffered, rose from the dead, and was glorified through the Spirit who sanctifies. To preach Christ means to feed the soul, make it righteous, set it free, and save it, provided it believes the preaching. Faith alone is the saving and efficacious use of the Word of God, according to Rom. 10[:9]: "If you confess with your lips that Jesus is Lord and believe in your heart that God raised him from the dead, you will be saved." Furthermore, "Christ is the end of the law, that every one who has faith may be justified" [Rom. 10:4]. Again, in Rom. 1[:17], "He who through faith is righteous shall live." The Word of

God cannot be received and cherished by any works whatever but only by faith. Therefore it is clear that, as the soul needs only the Word of God for its life and righteousness, so it is justified by faith alone and not any works; for if it could be justified by anything else, it would not need the Word, and consequently it would not need faith.

This faith cannot exist in connection with works—that is to say, if you at the same time claim to be justified by works, whatever their character—for that would be the same as "limping with two different opinions" [1 Kings 18:21], as worshiping Baal and kissing one's own hand [Job 31:27–28], which, as Job says, is a very great iniquity. Therefore the moment you begin to have faith you learn that all things in you are altogether blameworthy, sinful, and damnable, as the Apostle says in Rom. 3[:23], "Since all have sinned and fall short of the glory of God," and, "None is righteous, no, not one; . . . all have turned aside, together they have gone wrong" (Rom. 3:10–12). When you have learned this you will know that you need Christ, who suffered and rose again for you so that, if you believe in him, you may through this faith become a new man in so far as your sins are forgiven and you are justified by the merits of another, namely, of Christ alone.

Since, therefore, this faith can rule only in the inner man, as Rom. 10[:10] says, "For man believes with his heart and so is justified," and since faith alone justifies, it is clear that the inner man cannot be justified, freed, or saved by any outer work or action at all, and that these works, whatever their character, have nothing to do with this inner man. On the other hand, only ungodliness and unbelief of heart, and no outer work, make him guilty and a damnable servant of sin. Wherefore it ought to be the first concern of every Christian to lay aside all confidence in works and increasingly to strengthen faith alone and through faith to grow in the knowledge, not of works, but of Christ Jesus, who suffered and rose for him, as Peter teaches in the last chapter of his first Epistle (1 Pet. 5:10). No other work makes a Christian. Thus when the Jews asked Christ, as related in John 6[:28], what they must do "to be doing the work of God," he brushed aside the multitude of works which he saw they did in great profusion and suggested one work, saying, "This is the work of God, that you believe in him whom he has sent" [John 6:29]; "for on him has God the Father set his seal" [John 6:27].

Therefore true faith in Christ is a treasure beyond comparison which brings with it complete salvation and saves man from every evil, as Christ says in the last chapter of Mark [16:16]: "He who believes and is baptized will be saved; but he who does not believe will be condemned." Isaiah contemplated this treasure and foretold it in chapter 10: "The Lord will make a small and consuming word upon the land, and it will overflow with righteousness" [cf. Isa. 10:22]. This is as though he said, "Faith, which is a small and perfect fulfillment of the law, will fill believers with so great a righteousness that they will need nothing more to become righteous." So Paul says, Rom.

10[:10], "For man believes with his heart and so is justified."

Should you ask how it happens that faith alone justifies and offers us such a treasure of great benefits without works in view of the fact that so many works, ceremonies, and laws are prescribed in the Scriptures, I answer: First of all, remember what has been said, namely, that faith alone, without works, justifies, frees, and saves; we shall make this clearer later on. Here we must point out that the entire Scripture of God is divided into two parts: commandments and promises. Although the commandments teach things that are good, the things taught are not done as soon as they are taught, for the commandments show us what we ought to do but do not give us the power to do it. They are intended to teach man to know himself, that through them he may recognize his inability to do good and may despair of his own ability. That is why they are called the Old Testament and constitute the Old Testament. For example, the commandment, "You shall not covet"

[Exod. 20:17], is a command which proves us all to be sinners, for no one can avoid coveting no matter how much he may struggle against it. Therefore, in order not to covet and to fulfill the commandment, a man is compelled to despair of himself, to seek the help which he does not find in himself elsewhere and from someone else, as stated in Hosea [13:9]: "Destruction is your own, O Israel: your help is only in me." As we fare with respect to one commandment, so we fare with all, for it is equally impossible for us to keep any one of them.

Now when a man has learned through the commandments to recognize his helplessness and is distressed about how he might satisfy the law—since the law must be fulfilled so that not a jot or tittle shall be lost, otherwise man will be condemned without hope—then, being truly humbled and reduced to nothing in his own eyes, he finds in himself nothing whereby he may be justified and saved. Here the second part of Scripture comes to our aid, namely, the promises of God which declare the glory of God, saying,

"If you wish to fulfill the law and not covet, as the law demands, come, believe in Christ in whom grace, righteousness, peace, liberty, and all things are promised you. If you believe, you shall have all things; if you do not believe, you shall lack all things." That which is impossible for you to accomplish by trying to fulfill all the works of the law—many and useless as they all are—you will accomplish quickly and easily through faith. God our Father has made all things depend on faith so that whoever has faith will have everything, and whoever does not have faith will have nothing. "For God has consigned all men to disobedience, that he may have mercy upon all," as it is stated in Rom. 11[:32]. Thus the promises of God give what the commandments of God demand and fulfill what the law prescribes so that all things may be God's alone, both the commandments and the fulfilling of the commandments. He alone commands; he alone fulfills. Therefore the promises of God belong to the New Testament. Indeed, they are the New Testament.

Since these promises of God are holy, true, righteous, free, and peaceful words, full of goodness, the soul which clings to them with a firm faith will be so closely united with them and altogether absorbed by them that it not only will share in all their power but will be saturated and intoxicated by them. If a touch of Christ healed, how much more will this most tender spiritual touch, this absorbing of the Word, communicate to the soul all things that belong to the Word. This, then, is how through faith alone without works the soul is justified by the Word of God, sanctified, made true, peaceful, and free, filled with every blessing and truly made a child of God, as John 1[:12] says: "But to all who . . . believed in his name, he gave power to become children of God."

From what has been said it is easy to see from what source faith derives such great power and why a good work or all good works together cannot equal it. No good work can rely upon the Word of God or live in the soul, for faith alone and the Word of God rule in the soul. Just as the heated iron glows like fire because of the union of fire with it, so the Word imparts its qualities to the soul. It is clear, then, that a Christian has all that he needs in faith and needs no works to justify him; and if he has no need of works, he has no need of the law; and if he has no need of the law, surely he is free from the law. It is true that "the law is not laid down for the just" [1 Tim. 1:9]. This is that Christian liberty, our faith, which does not induce us to live in idleness or wickedness but makes the law and works unnecessary for any man's righteousness and salvation.

This is the first power of faith. Let us now examine also the second. It is a further function of faith that it honors him whom it trusts with the most reverent and highest regard since it considers him truthful and trustworthy. There is no other honor equal to the estimate of truthfulness and righteousness with which we honor him whom we trust. Could we ascribe to a man anything greater than truthfulness and righteousness and perfect goodness? On the other hand, there is no way in which we can show greater contempt for a man than to regard him as false and wicked and to be suspicious of him, as we do when we do not trust him. So when the soul firmly trusts God's promises, it regards him as truthful and righteous. Nothing more excellent than this can be ascribed to God. The very highest worship of God is this: that we ascribe to him truthfulness, righteousness, and whatever else should be ascribed to one who is trusted. When this is done, the soul consents to his will. Then it hallows his name and allows itself to be treated according to God's good pleasure, for, clinging to God's promises, it does not doubt that he who is true, just, and wise will do, dispose, and provide all things well.

Is not such a soul most obedient to God in all things by this faith? What commandment is there that such obedience has not completely fulfilled? What more complete fulfillment is there than obedience in all things? This obedience, however, is not rendered by works, but by faith alone. On the other hand, what greater rebellion against God, what greater wickedness, what greater contempt of God is there than not believing his promise? For what is this but to make God a liar or to doubt that he is truthful?—that is, to ascribe truthfulness to one's self but lying and vanity to God? Does not a man who does this deny God and set himself up as an idol in his heart? Then of what good are works done in such wickedness, even if they were the works of angels and apostles? Therefore God has rightly included all things, not under anger or lust, but under unbelief, so that they who imagine that they are fulfilling the law by doing the works of chastity and mercy required by the law (the civil and human virtues) might not be saved. They are included under the sin of unbelief and must either seek mercy or be justly condemned.

When, however, God sees that we consider him truth and by the faith of our heart pay him the great honor which is due him, he does us that great honor of considering us truthful and righteous for the sake of our faith. Faith works truth and righteousness by giving God what belongs to him. Therefore God in turn glorifies our righteousness. It is true and just that God is truthful and just, and to consider and confess him to be so is the same as being truthful and just. Accordingly he says in 1 Sam. 2[:30], "Those who honor me I will honor, and those who despise me shall be lightly esteemed." So Paul says in Rom. 4[:3] that Abraham's faith "was reckoned to him as righteousness" because by it he gave glory most perfectly to God, and that for the same reason our faith shall be reckoned to us as righteousness if we believe.

The third incomparable benefit of faith is that it unites the soul with Christ as a bride is united with her bridegroom. By this mystery, as the Apostle teaches, Christ and the soul become one flesh [Eph. 5:31–32]. And if they are one flesh and there is between them a true marriage—indeed the most perfect of all marriages, since human marriages are but poor examples of this one true marriage—it follows that everything they have they hold in common, the good as well as the evil. Accordingly the believing soul can boast of and glory in whatever Christ has as though it were its own, and whatever the soul has Christ claims as his own. Let us compare these and we shall see inestimable benefits. Christ is full of grace, life, and salvation. The soul is full of sins, death, and damnation. Now let faith come between them and sins, death, and damnation will be Christ's, while grace, life, and salvation will be the soul's; for if Christ is a bridegroom, he must take upon himself the things which are his bride's and bestow upon her the things that are his. If he gives her his body and very self, how shall he not give her all that is his? And if he takes the body of the bride, how shall he not take all that is hers?

Here we have a most pleasing vision not only of communion but of a blessed struggle and victory and salvation and redemption. Christ is God and man in one person. He has neither sinned nor died, and is not condemned, and he cannot sin, die, or be condemned; his righteousness, life, and salvation are unconquerable, eternal, omnipotent. By the wedding ring of faith he shares in the sins, death, and pains of hell which are his bride's. As a matter of fact, he makes them his own and acts as if they were his own and as if he himself had sinned; he suffered, died, and descended into hell that he might overcome them all. Now since it was such a one who did all this, and death and hell could not swallow him up, these were necessarily swallowed up by him in a mighty duel; for his righteousness is greater than the sins of all men, his life stronger than death, his salvation more invincible than hell. Thus the believing soul by means of the pledge of its faith is free in Christ, its bridegroom, free from all sins, secure against death and hell, and is endowed with the eternal righteousness, life, and salvation of Christ its bridegroom. So he takes to himself a glorious bride, "without spot or wrinkle, cleansing her by the washing of water with the word" [cf. Eph. 5:26–27] of life, that is, by faith in the Word of life, righteousness, and salvation. In this way he marries her in faith, steadfast love, and in mercies, righteousness, and justice, as Hos. 2[:19–20] says.

Who then can fully appreciate what this royal marriage means? Who can understand the riches of the glory of this grace? Here this rich and divine bridegroom Christ marries this poor, wicked harlot, redeems her from all her evil, and adorns her with all his goodness. Her sins cannot now destroy her, since they are laid upon Christ and swallowed up by him. And she has that righteousness in Christ, her husband, of which she may boast as of her own and which she can confidently display alongside her sins in the face of death and hell and say, "If I have sinned, yet my Christ, in whom I believe, has not sinned, and all his is mine and all mine is his," as the bride in the Song of Solomon [2:16] says, "My beloved is mine and I am his." This is what Paul means when he says in 1 Cor. 15[:57], "Thanks be to God, who gives us the victory through our Lord Jesus Christ," that is, the victory over sin and death, as he also says there, "The sting of death is sin, and the power of sin is the law" [1 Cor. 15:56].

From this you once more see that much is ascribed to faith, namely, that it alone can fulfill the law and justify without works. You see that the First Commandment, which says, "You shall worship one God," is fulfilled by faith alone. Though you were nothing but good works from the soles of your feet to the crown of your head, you would still not be righteous or worship God or fulfill the First Commandment, since God cannot be worshiped unless you ascribe to him the glory of truthfulness and all goodness which is due him. This cannot be done by works but only by the faith of the heart. Not by the doing of works but by believing do we glorify God and acknowledge that he is truthful. Therefore faith alone is the righteousness of a Christian and the fulfilling of all the commandments, for he who fulfills the First Commandment has no difficulty in fulfilling all the rest.

But works, being inanimate things, cannot glorify God, although they can, if faith is present, be done to the glory of

God. Here, however, we are not inquiring what works and what kind of works are done, but who it is that does them, who glorifies God and brings forth the works. This is done by faith which dwells in the heart and is the source and substance of all our righteousness. Therefore it is a blind and dangerous doctrine which teaches that the commandments must be fulfilled by works. The commandments must be fulfilled before any works can be done, and the works proceed from the fulfillment of the commandments [Rom. 13:10], as we shall hear.

That we may examine more profoundly that grace which our inner man has in Christ, we must realize that in the Old Testament God consecrated to himself all the first-born males. The birthright was highly prized for it involved a twofold honor, that of priesthood and that of kingship. The first-born brother was priest and lord over all the others and a type of Christ, the true and only first-born of God the Father and the Virgin Mary and true king and priest, but not after the fashion of the flesh and the world, for his kingdom is not of this world [John 18:36]. He reigns in heavenly and spiritual things and consecrates them—things such as righteousness, truth, wisdom, peace, salvation, etc. This does not mean that all things on earth and in hell are not also subject to him—otherwise how could he protect and save us from them?—but that his kingdom consists neither in them nor of them. Nor does his priesthood consist in the outer splendor of robes and postures like those of the human priesthood of Aaron and our present-day church; but it consists of spiritual things through which he by an invisible service intercedes for us in heaven before God, there offers himself as a sacrifice, and does all things a priest should do, as Paul describes him under the type of Melchizedek in the Epistle to the Hebrews [Heb. 6–7]. Nor does he only pray and intercede for us but he teaches us inwardly through the living instruction of his Spirit, thus performing the two real functions of a priest, of which the prayers and the preaching of human priests are visible types.

Now just as Christ by his birthright obtained these two prerogatives, so he imparts them to and shares them with everyone who believes in him according to the law of the above-mentioned marriage, according to which the wife owns whatever belongs to the husband. Hence all of us who believe in Christ are priests and kings in Christ, as 1 Pet. 2[:9] says: "You are a chosen race, God's own people, a royal priesthood, a priestly kingdom, that you may declare the wonderful deeds of him who called you out of darkness into his marvelous light."

The nature of this priesthood and kingship is something like this: First, with respect to the kingship, every Christian is by faith so exalted above all things that, by virtue of a spiritual power, he is lord of all things without exception, so that nothing can do him any harm. As a matter of fact, all things are made subject to him and are compelled to serve him in obtaining salvation. Accordingly Paul says in Rom. 8[:28], "All things work together for good for the elect," and in 1 Cor. 3[:21–23],

"All things are yours whether . . . life or death or the present or the future, all are yours; and you are Christ's. . . ." This is not to say that every Christian is placed over all things to have and control them by physical power—a madness with which some churchmen are afflicted—for such power belongs to kings, princes, and other men on earth. Our ordinary experience in life shows us that we are subjected to all, suffer many things, and even die. As a matter of fact, the more Christian a man is, the more evils, sufferings, and deaths he must endure, as we see in Christ the first-born prince himself, and in all his brethren, the saints. The power of which we speak is spiritual. It rules in the midst of enemies and is powerful in the midst of oppression. This means nothing else than that "power is made perfect in weakness" [2 Cor. 12:9] and that in all things I can find profit toward salvation [Rom. 8:28], so that the cross and death itself are compelled to serve me and to work together with me for my salvation. This is a splendid privilege and hard to attain, a truly omnipotent power, a spiritual dominion in which there is nothing so good and nothing so evil but that it shall work together for good to me, if only I believe. Yes, since faith alone suffices for salvation, I need nothing except faith exercising the power and dominion of its own liberty. Lo, this is the inestimable power and liberty of Christians.

Not only are we the freest of kings, we are also priests forever, which is far more excellent than being kings, for as priests we are worthy to appear before God to pray for others and to teach one another divine things. These are the functions of priests, and they cannot be granted to any unbeliever. Thus Christ has made it possible for us, provided we believe in him, to be not only his brethren, co-heirs, and fellow-kings, but also his fellow-priests. Therefore we may boldly come into the presence of God in the spirit of faith [Heb. 10:19, 22] and cry "Abba, Father!" pray for one another, and do all things which we see done and foreshadowed in the outer and visible works of priests.

He, however, who does not believe is not served by anything. On the contrary, nothing works for his good, but he himself is a servant of all, and all things turn out badly for him because he wickedly uses them to his own advantage and not to the glory of God. So he is no priest but a wicked man whose prayer becomes sin and who never comes into the presence of God because God does not hear sinners [John 9:31]. Who then can comprehend the lofty dignity of the Christian? By virtue of his royal power he rules over all things, death, life, and sin, and through his priestly glory is omnipotent with God because he does the things which God asks and desires, as it is written, "He will fulfill the desire of those who fear him; he also will hear their cry and save them" [cf. Phil. 4:13]. To this glory a man attains, certainly not by any works of his, but by faith alone.

From this anyone can clearly see how a Christian is free from all things and over all things so that he needs no works to make him righteous and save him, since faith alone abundantly confers all these

things. Should he grow so foolish, however, as to presume to become righteous,
free, saved, and a Christian by means of
some good work, he would instantly lose
faith and all its benefits, a foolishness
aptly illustrated in the fable of the dog
who runs along a stream with a piece of
meat in his mouth and, deceived by the
reflection of the meat in the water, opens
his mouth to snap at it and so loses both
the meat and the reflection.

You will ask, "If all who are in the
church are priests, how do these whom
we now call priests differ from laymen?"
I answer: Injustice is done those words
"priest," "cleric," "spiritual," "ecclesias-
tic," when they are transferred from all
Christians to those few who are now by a
mischievous usage called "ecclesiastics."
Holy Scripture makes no distinction between them, although it gives the name
"ministers," "servants," "stewards" to
those who are now proudly called popes,
bishops, and lords and who should according to the ministry of the Word serve
others and teach them the faith of Christ
and the freedom of believers. Although

we are all equally priests, we cannot all
publicly minister and teach. We ought
not to do so even if we could. Paul writes
accordingly in 1 Cor. 4 [1], "This is how
one should regard us, as servants of
Christ and stewards of the mysteries of
God."

That stewardship, however, has now
been developed into so great a display of
power and so terrible a tyranny that no
heathen empire or other earthly power
can be compared with it, just as if laymen
were not also Christians. Through this
perversion the knowledge of Christian
grace, faith, liberty, and of Christ himself
has altogether perished, and its place has
been taken by an unbearable bondage of
human works and laws until we have become, as the Lamentations of Jeremiah
[1] say, servants of the vilest men on
earth who abuse our misfortune to serve
only their base and shameless will.

To return to our purpose, I believe that
it has now become clear that it is not
enough or in any sense Christian to
preach the works, life, and words of
Christ as historical facts, as if the knowl-

edge of these would suffice for the conduct of life; yet this is the fashion among
those who must today be regarded as our
best preachers. Far less is it sufficient or
Christian to say nothing at all about
Christ and to teach instead the laws of
men and the decrees of the fathers. Now
there are not a few who preach Christ and
read about him that they may move
men's affections to sympathy with Christ,
to anger against the Jews, and such childish and effeminate nonsense. Rather
ought Christ to be preached to the end
that faith in him may be established that
he may not only be Christ, but be Christ
for you and me, and that what is said of
him and is denoted in his name may be
effectual in us. Such faith is produced
and preserved in us by preaching why
Christ came, what he brought and bestowed, what benefit it is to us to accept
him. This is done when that Christian liberty which he bestows is rightly taught
and we are told in what way we Christians are all kings and priests and therefore lords of all and may firmly believe
that whatever we have done is pleasing

and acceptable in the sight of God, as I have already said.

What man is there whose heart, upon hearing these things, will not rejoice to its depth, and when receiving such comfort will not grow tender so that he will love Christ as he never could by means of any laws or works? Who would have the power to harm or frighten such a heart? If the knowledge of sin or the fear of death should break in upon it, it is ready to hope in the Lord. It does not grow afraid when it hears tidings of evil. It is not disturbed when it sees its enemies. This is so because it believes that the righteousness of Christ is its own and that its sin is not its own, but Christ's, and that all sin is swallowed up by the righteousness of Christ. This, as has been said above, is a necessary consequence on account of faith in Christ. So the heart learns to scoff at death and sin and to say with the Apostle, "O death, where is thy victory? O death, where is thy sting? The sting of death is sin, and the power of sin is the law. But thanks be to God, who gives us the victory through our Lord Jesus Christ"

[1 Cor. 15:55–57]. Death is swallowed up not only in the victory of Christ but also by our victory, because through faith his victory has become ours and in that faith we also are conquerors.

Let this suffice concerning the inner man, his liberty, and the source of his liberty, the righteousness of faith. He needs neither laws nor good works but, on the contrary, is injured by them if he believes that he is justified by them.

Now let us turn to the second part, the outer man. Here we shall answer all those who, offended by the word "faith" and by all that has been said, now ask, "If faith does all things and is alone sufficient unto righteousness, why then are good works commanded? We will take our ease and do no works and be content with faith." I answer: not so, you wicked men, not so. That would indeed be proper if we were wholly inner and perfectly spiritual men. But such we shall be only at the last day, the day of the resurrection of the dead. As long as we live in the flesh we only begin to make some progress in that which shall be perfected in the future life.

For this reason the Apostle in Rom. 8[:23] calls all that we attain in this life "the first fruits of the Spirit" because we shall indeed receive the greater portion, even the fullness of the Spirit, in the future. This is the place to assert that which was said above, namely, that a Christian is the servant of all and made subject to all. Insofar as he is free he does no works, but insofar as he is a servant he does all kinds of works. How this is possible we shall see.

Although, as I have said, a man is abundantly and sufficiently justified by faith inwardly, in his spirit, and so has all that he needs, except insofar as this faith and these riches must grow from day to day even to the future life; yet he remains in this mortal life on earth. In this life he must control his own body and have dealings with men. Here the works begin; here a man cannot enjoy leisure; here he must indeed take care to discipline his body by fastings, watchings, labors, and other reasonable discipline and to subject it to the Spirit so that it will obey and conform to the inner man and faith and not revolt against faith and hinder the inner man, as it is the nature of the body to do if it is not held in check. The inner man, who by faith is created in the image of God, is both joyful and happy because of Christ in whom so many benefits are conferred upon him; and therefore it is his one occupation to serve God joyfully and without thought of gain, in love that is not constrained.

While he is doing this, behold, he meets a contrary will in his own flesh which strives to serve the world and seeks its own advantage. This the spirit of faith cannot tolerate, but with joyful zeal it attempts to put the body under control and hold it in check, as Paul says in Rom. 7[:22–23], "For I delight in the law of God, in my inmost self, but I see in my members another law at war with the law of my mind and making me captive to the law of sin," and in another place, "But I pommel my body and subdue it, lest after preaching to others I myself should be disqualified" [1 Cor. 9:27], and in Galatians [5:24], "And those who belong to Christ Jesus have crucified the flesh with its passions and desires."

In doing these works, however, we must not think that a man is justified before God by them, for faith, which alone is righteousness before God, cannot endure that erroneous opinion. We must, however, realize that these works reduce the body to subjection and purify it of its evil lusts, and our whole purpose is to be directed only toward the driving out of lusts. Since by faith the soul is cleansed and made to love God, it desires that all things, and especially its own body, shall be purified so that all things may join with it in loving and praising God. Hence a man cannot be idle, for the need of his body drives him and he is compelled to do many good works to reduce it to subjection. Nevertheless the works themselves do not justify him before God, but he does the works out of spontaneous love in obedience to God and considers nothing except the approval of God, whom he would most scrupulously obey in all things.

In this way everyone will easily be able to learn for himself the limit and discretion, as they say, of his bodily castigations, for he will fast, watch, and labor as much as he finds sufficient to repress the lasciviousness and lust of his body. But those who presume to be justified by works do not regard the mortifying of the lusts, but only the works themselves, and think that if only they have done as many and as great works as are possible, they have done well and have become righteous. At times they even addle their brains and destroy, or at least render useless, their natural strength with their works. This is the height of folly and utter ignorance of Christian life and faith, that a man should seek to be justified and saved by works and without faith.

In order to make that which we have said more easily understood, we shall explain by analogies. We should think of the works of a Christian who is justified and saved by faith because of the pure and free mercy of God, just as we would think of the works which Adam and Eve did in Paradise, and all their children would have done if they had not sinned. We read in Gen. 2[:15] that "The Lord God took the man and put him in the garden of Eden to till it and keep it." Now Adam was created righteous and upright and without sin by God so that he had no need of being justified and made upright through his tilling and keeping the garden; but, that he might not be idle, the Lord gave him a task to do, to cultivate and protect the garden. This task would truly have been the freest of works, done only to please God and not to obtain righteousness, which Adam already had in full measure and which would have been the birthright of us all.

The works of a believer are like this. Through his faith he has been restored to Paradise and created anew, has no need of works that he may become or be righteous; but that he may not be idle and may provide for and keep his body, he must do such works freely only to please God. Since, however, we are not wholly recreated, and our faith and love are not yet perfect, these are to be increased, not by external works, however, but of themselves.

A second example: A bishop, when he consecrates a church, confirms children, or performs some other duty belonging to his office, is not made a bishop by these works. Indeed, if he had not first been made a bishop, none of these works would be valid. They would be foolish, childish, and farcical. So the Christian who is consecrated by his faith does good works, but the works do not make him holier or more Christian, for that is the work of faith alone. And if a man were not first a believer and a Christian, all his works would amount to nothing and would be truly wicked and damnable sins.

The following statements are therefore true: "Good works do not make a good man, but a good man does good works; evil works do not make a wicked man, but a wicked man does evil works." Consequently it is always necessary that the substance or person himself be good before there can be any good works, and that good works follow and proceed from the good person, as Christ also says, "A good tree cannot bear evil fruit, nor can a bad tree bear good fruit" [Matt. 7:18]. It is clear that the fruits do not bear the tree

and that the tree does not grow on the
fruits, also that, on the contrary, the trees
bear the fruits and the fruits grow on the
trees. As it is necessary, therefore, that the
trees exist before their fruits and the
fruits do not make trees either good or
bad, but rather as the trees are, so are the
fruits they bear; so a man must first be
good or wicked before he does a good or
wicked work, and his works do not make
him good or wicked, but he himself
makes his works either good or wicked.

Illustrations of the same truth can be
seen in all trades. A good or a bad house
does not make a good or a bad builder;
but a good or a bad builder makes a good
or a bad house. And in general, the work
never makes the workman like itself, but
the workman makes the work like himself. So it is with the works of man. As the
man is, whether believer or unbeliever, so
also is his work—good if it was done in
faith, wicked if it was done in unbelief.
But the converse is not true, that the work
makes the man either a believer or an unbeliever. As works do not make a man a
believer, so also they do not make him

righteous. But as faith makes a man a believer and righteous, so faith does good works. Since, then, works justify no one, and a man must be righteous before he does a good work, it is very evident that it is faith alone which, because of the pure mercy of God through Christ and in his Word, worthily and sufficiently justifies and saves the person. A Christian has no need of any work or law in order to be saved since through faith he is free from every law and does everything out of pure liberty and freely. He seeks neither benefit nor salvation since he already abounds in all things and is saved through the grace of God because in his faith he now seeks only to please God.

Furthermore, no good work helps justify or save an unbeliever. On the other hand, no evil work makes him wicked or damns him; but the unbelief which makes the person and the tree evil does the evil and damnable works. Hence when a man is good or evil, this is effected not by the works, but by faith or unbelief, as the Wise Man says, "This is the beginning of sin, that a man falls away from God" [cf.

Sir. 10:14–15], which happens when he does not believe. And Paul says in Heb. 11[:6], "For whoever would draw near to God must believe. . . ." And Christ says the same: "Either make the tree good, and its fruit good; or make the tree bad, and its fruit bad" [Matt. 12:33], as if he would say, "Let him who wishes to have good fruit begin by planting a good tree." So let him who wishes to do good works begin not with the doing of works, but with believing, which makes the person good, for nothing makes a man good except faith, or evil except unbelief.

It is indeed true that in the sight of men a man is made good or evil by his works; but this being made good or evil only means that the man who is good or evil is pointed out and known as such, as Christ says in Matt. 7[:20], "Thus you will know them by their fruits." All this remains on the surface, however, and very many have been deceived by this outward appearance and have presumed to write and teach concerning good works by which we may be justified without even mentioning faith. They go their way, always being deceived and deceiving [2 Tim. 3:13], progressing, indeed, but into a worse state, blind leaders of the blind, wearying themselves with many works and still never attaining to true righteousness [Matt. 15:14]. Of such people Paul says in 2 Tim. 3:[5, 7], "Holding the form of religion but denying the power of it . . . who will listen to anybody and can never arrive at a knowledge of the truth."

Whoever, therefore, does not wish to go astray with those blind men must look beyond works, and beyond laws and doctrines about works. Turning his eyes from works, he must look upon the person and ask how he is justified. For the person is justified and saved, not by works or laws, but by the Word of God, that is, by the promise of his grace, and by faith, that the glory may remain God's, who saved us not by works of righteousness which we have done [Titus 3:5], but by virtue of his mercy by the word of his grace when we believed [1 Cor. 1:21].

From this it is easy to know how far good works are to be rejected or not, and by what standard all the teachings of men concerning works are to be interpreted. If works are sought after as a means to righteousness, are burdened with this perverse leviathan, and are done under the false impression that through them one is justified, they are made necessary and freedom and faith are destroyed; and this addition to them makes them no longer good but truly damnable works. They are not free, and they blaspheme the grace of God since to justify and to save by faith belongs to the grace of God alone. What the works have no power to do they nevertheless—by a godless presumption through this folly of ours—pretend to do and thus violently force themselves into the office and glory of grace. We do not, therefore, reject good works; on the contrary, we cherish and teach them as much as possible. We do not condemn them for their own sake but on account of this godless addition to them and the perverse idea that righteousness is to be sought through them; for that makes them appear good outwardly, when in truth they are not good. They deceive men and lead them to deceive one another like ravening wolves in sheep's clothing [Matt. 7:15].

But this leviathan, or perverse notion concerning works, is unconquerable where sincere faith is wanting. Those work-saints cannot get rid of it unless faith, its destroyer, comes and rules in their hearts. Nature of itself cannot drive it out or even recognize it, but rather regards it as a mark of the most holy will. If the influence of custom is added and confirms this perverseness of nature, as wicked teachers have caused it to do, it becomes an incurable evil and leads astray and destroys countless men beyond all hope of restoration. Therefore, although it is good to preach and write about penitence, confession, and satisfaction, our teaching is unquestionably deceitful and diabolical if we stop with that and do not go on to teach about faith.

Christ, like his forerunner John, not only said, "Repent" [Matt. 3:2; 4:17], but added the word of faith, saying, "The kingdom of heaven is at hand." We are not to preach only one of these words of God, but both; we are to bring forth out of our treasure things new and old, the voice of the law as well as the word of grace [Matt. 13:52]. We must bring forth the voice of the law that men may be made to fear and come to a knowledge of their sins and so be converted to repentance and a better life. But we must not stop with that, for that would only amount to wounding and not binding up, smiting and not healing, killing and not making alive, leading down into hell and not bringing back again, humbling and not exalting. Therefore we must also preach the word of grace and the promise of forgiveness by which faith is taught and aroused. Without this word of grace the works of the law, contrition, penitence, and all the rest are done and taught in vain.

Preachers of repentance and grace remain even to our day, but they do not explain God's law and promise that a man might learn from them the source of repentance and grace. Repentance proceeds from the law of God, but faith or grace from the promise of God, as Rom. 10[:17] says: "So faith comes from what is heard, and what is heard comes by the preaching of Christ." Accordingly man is consoled and exalted by faith in the divine promise after he has been humbled and led to a knowledge of himself by the threats and the fear of the divine law. So we read in Ps. 30[:5]: "Weeping may tarry for the night, but joy comes with the morning."

Let this suffice concerning works in general and at the same time concerning the works which a Christian does for himself. Lastly, we shall also speak of the things which he does toward his neighbor. A man does not live for himself alone in this mortal body to work for it alone, but he lives also for all men on earth; rather, he lives only for others and not for himself. To this end he brings his body into subjection that he may the more sincerely and freely serve others, as Paul says in Rom. 14[:7–8], "None of us lives to himself, and none of us dies to himself. If we live, we live to the Lord, and if we die, we die to the Lord." He cannot ever in this life be idle and without works toward his neighbors, for he will

necessarily speak, deal with, and ex-
change views with men, as Christ also,
being made in the likeness of men [Phil.
2:7], was found in form as a man and
conversed with men, as Bar. 3[:38] says.

Man, however, needs none of these
things for his righteousness and salvation. Therefore he should be guided in all
his works by this thought and contem-
plate this one thing alone, that he may
serve and benefit others in all that he
does, considering nothing except the
need and the advantage of his neighbor.
Accordingly the Apostle commands us to
work with our hands so that we may give
to the needy, although he might have said
that we should work to support ourselves.
He says, however, "that he may be able to
give to those in need" [Eph. 4:28]. This is
what makes caring for the body a Christian work, that through its health and
comfort we may be able to work, to acquire, and to lay by funds with which to
aid those who are in need, that in this
way the strong member may serve the
weaker, and we may be sons of God, each
eating for and working for the other,

bearing one another's burdens and so fulfilling the law of Christ [Gal. 6:2]. This is a truly Christian life. Here faith is truly active through love [Gal. 5:6], that is, it finds expression in works of the freest service, cheerfully and lovingly done, with which a man willingly serves another without hope of reward; and for himself he is satisfied with the fullness and wealth of his faith.

Accordingly Paul, after teaching the Philippians how rich they were made through faith in Christ, in which they obtained all things, thereafter teaches them, saying, "So if there is any encouragement in Christ, any incentive of love, any participation in the Spirit, any affection and sympathy, complete my joy by being of the same mind, having the same love, being in full accord and of one mind. Do nothing from selfishness or conceit, but in humility count others better than yourselves. Let each of you look not only to his own interests, but also to the interests of others" [Phil. 2:1–4]. Here we see clearly that the Apostle has prescribed this rule for the life of Christians, namely, that we should devote all our works to the welfare of others, since each has such abundant riches in his faith that all his other works and his whole life are a surplus with which he can by voluntary benevolence serve and do good to his neighbor.

As an example of such life the Apostle cites Christ, saying, "Have this mind among yourselves, which you have in Christ Jesus, who, though he was in the form of God, did not count equality with God a thing to be grasped, but emptied himself, taking the form of a servant, being born in the likeness of men. And being found in human form he humbled himself and became obedient unto death" [Phil. 2:5–8]. This salutary word of the Apostle has been obscured for us by those who have not at all understood his words, "form of God," "form of a servant," "human form," "likeness of men," and have applied them to the divine and the human nature. Paul means this: Although Christ was filled with the form of God and rich in all good things, so that he needed no work and no suffering to make him righteous and saved (for he had all this eternally), yet he was not puffed up by them and did not exalt himself above us and assume power over us, although he could rightly have done so; but, on the contrary, he so lived, labored, worked, suffered, and died that he might be like other men and in fashion and in actions be nothing else than a man, just as if he had need of all these things and had nothing of the form of God. But he did all this for our sake, that he might serve us and that all things which he accomplished in this form of a servant might become ours.

So a Christian, like Christ his head, is filled and made rich by faith and should be content with this form of God which he has obtained by faith; only, as I have said, he should increase this faith until it is made perfect. For this faith is his life, his righteousness, and his salvation: it saves him and makes him acceptable, and bestows upon him all things that are Christ's, as has been said above, and as Paul asserts in Gal. 2[:20] when he says, "And the life I now live in the flesh I live by faith in the Son of God." Although the Christian is thus free from all works, he ought in this liberty to empty himself, take upon himself the form of a servant, be made in the likeness of men, be found in human form, and to serve, help, and in every way deal with his neighbor as he sees that God through Christ has dealt and still deals with him. This he should do freely, having regard for nothing but divine approval.

He ought to think: "Although I am an unworthy and condemned man, my God has given me in Christ all the riches of righteousness and salvation without any merit on my part, out of pure, free mercy, so that from now on I need nothing except faith which believes that this is true. Why should I not therefore freely, joyfully, with all my heart, and with an eager will do all things which I know are pleasing and acceptable to such a Father who has overwhelmed me with his inestimable riches? I will therefore give myself as a Christ to my neighbor, just as Christ offered himself to me; I will do nothing in this life except what I see is necessary, profitable, and salutary to my neighbor, since through faith I have an abundance of all good things in Christ."

Behold, from faith thus flow forth love and joy in the Lord, and from love a joyful, willing, and free mind that serves one's neighbor willingly and takes no account of gratitude or ingratitude, of praise or blame, of gain or loss. For a man does not serve that he may put men under obligations. He does not distinguish between friends and enemies or anticipate their thankfulness or unthankfulness, but he most freely and most willingly spends himself and all that he has, whether he wastes all on the thankless or whether he gains a reward. As his Father does, distributing all things to all men richly and freely, making "his sun rise on the evil and on the good" [Matt. 5:45], so also the son does all things and suffers all things with that freely bestowing joy which is his delight when through Christ he sees it in God, the dispenser of such great benefits.

Therefore, if we recognize the great and precious things which are given us, as Paul says [Rom. 5:5], our hearts will be filled by the Holy Spirit with the love which makes us free, joyful, almighty workers and conquerors over all tribulations, servants of our neighbors, and yet lords of all. For those who do not recognize the gifts bestowed upon them through Christ, however, Christ has been born in vain; they go their way with their works and shall never come to taste or feel those things. Just as our neighbor is in need and lacks that in which we abound, so we were in need before God and lacked his mercy. Hence, as our heavenly Father has in Christ freely come to our aid, we also ought freely to help our neighbor through our body and its works, and each one should become as it were a Christ to the other that we may be Christs to one another and Christ may be the same in all, that is, that we may be truly Christians.

Who then can comprehend the riches and the glory of the Christian life? It can do all things and has all things and lacks nothing. It is lord over sin, death, and hell, and yet at the same time it serves, ministers to, and benefits all men. But

alas in our day this life is unknown
throughout the world; it is neither
preached about nor sought after; we are
altogether ignorant of our own name and
do not know why we are Christians or
bear the name of Christians. Surely we
are named after Christ, not because he is
absent from us, but because he dwells in
us, that is, because we believe in him and
are Christs one to another and do to our
neighbors as Christ does to us. But in our
day we are taught by the doctrine of men
to seek nothing but merits, rewards, and
the things that are ours; of Christ we have
made only a taskmaster far harsher than
Moses.

We have a pre-eminent example of
such a faith in the blessed Virgin. As is
written in Luke 2[:22], she was purified
according to the law of Moses according
to the custom of all women, although she
was not bound by that law and did not
need to be purified. Out of free and willing love, however, she submitted to the
law like other women that she might not
offend or despise them. She was not justified by this work, but being righteous

she did it freely and willingly. So also our works should be done, not that we may be justified by them, since, being justified beforehand by faith, we ought to do all things freely and joyfully for the sake of others.

St. Paul also circumcised his disciple Timothy, not because circumcision was necessary for his righteousness, but that he might not offend or despise the Jews who were weak in the faith and could not yet grasp the liberty of faith. But, on the other hand, when they despised the liberty of faith and insisted that circumcision was necessary for righteousness, he resisted them and did not allow Titus to be circumcised (Gal. 2[:3]). Just as he was unwilling to offend or despise any man's weak faith and yielded to their will for a time, so he was also unwilling that the liberty of faith should be offended against or despised by stubborn, work-righteous men. He chose a middle way, sparing the weak for a time, but always withstanding the stubborn, that he might convert all to the liberty of faith. What

we do should be done with the same zeal
to sustain the weak in faith, as in Rom.
14[:1]; but we should firmly resist the
stubborn teachers of works. Of this we
shall say more later.

Christ also, in Matt. 17[:24–27], when
the tax money was demanded of his dis-
ciples, discussed with St. Peter whether
the sons of the king were not free from
the payment of tribute, and Peter af-
firmed that they were. Nonetheless, Christ
commanded Peter to go to the sea and
said, "Not to give offense to them, go to
the sea and cast a hook, and take the first
fish that comes up, and when you open
its mouth you will find a shekel; take that
and give it to them for me and for yourself." This incident fits our subject beautifully for Christ here calls himself and
those who are his children sons of the
king, who need nothing; and yet he freely
submits and pays the tribute. Just as necessary and helpful as this work was to
Christ's righteousness or salvation, just so
much do all other works of his or his followers avail for righteousness, since they

all follow after righteousness and are free and are done only to serve others and to give them an example of good works.

Of the same nature are the precepts which Paul gives in Rom. 13[:1-7], namely, that Christians should be subject to the governing authorities and be ready to do every good work, not that they shall in this way be justified, since they already are righteous through faith, but that in the liberty of the Spirit they shall by so doing serve others and the authorities themselves and obey their will freely and out of love. The works of all colleges, monasteries, and priests should be of this nature. Each one should do the works of his profession and station, not that by them he may strive after righteousness, but that through them he may keep his body under control, be an example to others who also need to keep their bodies under control, and finally that by such works he may submit his will to that of others in the freedom of love. But very great care must always be exercised so that no man in a false confidence imag-

ines that by such works he will be justified or acquire merit or be saved; for this
is the work of faith alone, as I have re-
peatedly said.

Anyone knowing this could easily and
without danger find his way through
those numberless mandates and precepts
of pope, bishops, monasteries, churches,
princes, and magistrates upon which
some ignorant pastors insist as if they
were necessary to righteousness and salvation, calling them "precepts of the
church," although they are nothing of the
kind. For a Christian, as a free man, will
say, "I will fast, pray, do this and that as
men command, not because it is necessary to my righteousness or salvation; but
that I may show due respect to the pope,
the bishop, the community, a magistrate,
or my neighbor, and give them an example. I will do and suffer all things, just as
Christ did and suffered far more for me,
although he needed nothing of it all for
himself, and was made under the law for
my sake, although he was not under the
law." Although tyrants do violence or

injustice in making their demands, yet it will do no harm as long as they demand nothing contrary to God.

From what has been said, everyone can pass a safe judgment on all works and laws and make a trustworthy distinction between them and know who are the blind and ignorant pastors and who are the good and true. Any work that is not done solely for the purpose of keeping the body under control or of serving one's neighbor, as long as he asks nothing contrary to God, is not good or Christian. For this reason I greatly fear that few or no colleges, monasteries, altars, and offices of the church are really Christian in our day—nor the special fasts and prayers on certain saints' days. I fear, I say, that in all these we seek only our profit, thinking that through them our sins are purged away and that we find salvation in them. In this way Christian liberty perishes altogether. This is a consequence of our ignorance of Christian faith and liberty.

This ignorance and suppression of liberty very many blind pastors take pains to encourage. They stir up and urge on their people in these practices by praising such works, puffing them up with their indulgences, and never teaching faith. If, however, you wish to pray, fast, or establish a foundation in the church, I advise you to be careful not to do it in order to obtain some benefit, whether temporal or eternal, for you would do injury to your faith which alone offers you all things. Your one care should be that faith may grow, whether it is trained by works or sufferings. Make your gifts freely and for no consideration, so that others may profit by them and fare well because of you and your goodness. In this way you shall be truly good and Christian. Of what benefit to you are the good works which you do not need for keeping your body under control? Your faith is sufficient for you, through which God has given you all things.

See, according to this rule the good things we have from God should flow from one to the other and be common to all, so that everyone should "put on" his neighbor and so conduct himself toward him as if he himself were in the other's place. From Christ the good things have flowed and are flowing into us. He has so "put on" us and acted for us as if he had been what we are. From us they flow on to those who have need of them so that I should lay before God my faith and my righteousness that they may cover and intercede for the sins of my neighbor which I take upon myself and so labor and serve in them as if they were my very own. That is what Christ did for us. This is true love and the genuine rule of a Christian life. Love is true and genuine where there is true and genuine faith. Hence the Apostle says of love in 1 Cor. 13[:5] that "it does not seek its own."

We conclude, therefore, that a Christian lives not in himself, but in Christ and in his neighbor. Otherwise he is not a Christian. He lives in Christ through faith, in his neighbor through love. By faith he is caught up beyond himself into God. By love he descends beneath himself into his neighbor. Yet he always remains in God and in his love, as Christ says in John 1[:51], "Truly, truly, I say to you, you will see heaven opened, and the angels of God ascending and descending upon the Son of man."

Enough now of freedom. As you see, it is a spiritual and true freedom and makes our hearts free from all sins, laws and commands, as Paul says, 1 Tim. 1[:9], "The law is not laid down for the just." It is more excellent than all other liberty, which is external, as heaven is more excellent than earth. May Christ give us this liberty both to understand and to preserve. Amen.

Finally, something must be added for the sake of those for whom nothing can be said so well that they will not spoil it by misunderstanding it. It is questionable whether they will understand even what will be said here. There are very many who, when they hear of this freedom of faith, immediately turn it into an occasion for the flesh and think that now all things are allowed them. They want to show that they are free men and Christians only by despising and finding fault with ceremonies, traditions, and human laws; as if they were Christians because on stated days they do not fast or eat meat when others fast, or because they do not use the accustomed prayers, and with upturned nose scoff at the precepts of men, although they utterly disregard all else that pertains to the Christian religion. The extreme opposite of these are those who rely for their salvation solely on their reverent observance of ceremonies, as if they would be saved because on certain days they fast or abstain from meats, or pray certain prayers; these make a boast of the precepts of the church and of the fathers, and do not care a fig for the things which are of the essence of our faith. Plainly, both are in error because they neglect the weightier things which are necessary to salvation, and quarrel so noisily about trifling and unnecessary matters.

How much better is the teaching of the Apostle Paul who bids us take a middle course and condemns both sides when he says, "Let not him who eats despise him who abstains, and let not him who abstains pass judgment on him who eats" [Rom. 14:3]. Here you see that they who neglect and disparage ceremonies, not out of piety, but out of mere contempt, are reproved, since the Apostle teaches us not to despise them. Such men are puffed up by knowledge. On the other hand, he teaches those who insist on the ceremonies not to judge the others, for neither party acts toward the other according to the love that edifies. Wherefore we ought to listen to Scripture which teaches that we should not go aside to the right or to the left [Deut. 28:14] but follow the statutes of the Lord which are right, "rejoicing the heart" [Ps. 19:8]. As a man is not righteous because he keeps and clings to the works and forms of the ceremonies, so also will a man not be counted righteous merely because he neglects and despises them.

Our faith in Christ does not free us from works but from false opinions concerning works, that is, from the foolish presumption that justification is acquired by works. Faith redeems, corrects, and preserves our consciences so that we know that righteousness does not consist in works, although works neither can nor ought to be wanting; just as we cannot be without food and drink and all the works of this mortal body, yet our righteousness is not in them, but in faith; and yet those works of the body are not to be despised or neglected on that account. In this world we are bound by the needs of our bodily life, but we are not righteous because of them. "My kingship is not of this world" [John 18:36], says Christ. He does not, however, say, "My kingship is not here, that is, in this world." And Paul says, "Though we live in the world we are not carrying on a worldly war" [2 Cor. 10:3], and in Gal. 2[:20], "The life I now live in the flesh I live by faith in the Son of God." Thus what we do, live, and are in works and ceremonies, we do because of the necessities of this life and of the effort to rule our body. Nevertheless we are righteous, not in these, but in the faith of the Son of God.

Hence the Christian must take a middle course and face those two classes of men. He will meet first the unyielding, stubborn ceremonialists who like deaf adders are not willing to hear the truth of liberty [Ps. 58:4] but, having no faith, boast of, prescribe, and insist upon their ceremonies as means of justification. Such were the Jews of old, who were unwilling to learn how to do good. These he must resist, do the very opposite, and offend them boldly lest by their impious views they drag many with them into error. In the presence of such men it is good to eat meat, break the fasts, and for the sake of the liberty of faith do other things which they regard as the greatest of sins. Of them we must say, "Let them alone; they are blind guides." According to this principle Paul would not circumcise Titus when the Jews insisted that he should [Gal. 2:3], and Christ excused the apostles when they plucked ears of grain on the sabbath [Matt. 12:1–8]. There are many similar instances. The other class of men whom a Christian will meet are the simple-minded, ignorant men, weak in the faith, as the Apostle calls them, who cannot yet grasp the liberty of faith, even if they were willing to do so [Rom. 14:1]. These he must take care not to offend. He must yield to their weakness until they are more fully instructed. Since they do and think as they do, not because they are stubbornly wicked, but only because their faith is weak, the fasts and other things which they consider necessary must be observed to avoid giving them offense. This is the command of love which would harm no one but would serve all men. It is not by their fault that they are weak, but by that of their pastors who have taken them captive with the snares of their traditions and have wickedly used these traditions as rods with which to beat them. They should have been delivered from these pastors by the teachings of faith and freedom. So the Apostle teaches us in Romans 14: "If food is a cause of my brother's falling, I will never eat meat" [cf. Rom. 14:21 and 1 Cor. 8:13]; and again, "I know and am persuaded in the Lord Jesus that nothing is unclean in itself; but it is unclean for any one who thinks it unclean" [Rom. 14:14].

For this reason, although we should boldly resist those teachers of traditions and sharply censure the laws of the popes by means of which they plunder the people of God, yet we must spare the timid multitude whom those impious tyrants hold captive by means of these laws until they are set free. Therefore fight strenuously against the wolves, but for the sheep and not also against the sheep. This you will do if you inveigh against the laws and the lawgivers and at the same time observe the laws with the weak so that they will not be offended, until they also recognize tyranny and understand their freedom. If you wish to use your freedom, do so in secret, as Paul says, Rom. 14[:22], "The faith that you have, keep between yourself and God"; but take care not to use your freedom in the sight of the weak. On the other hand, use your freedom constantly and consistently in the sight of and despite the tyrants and the stubborn so that they also may learn that they are impious, that their laws are of no avail for righteousness, and that they had no right to set them up.

Since we cannot live our lives without ceremonies and works, and the perverse and untrained youth need to be restrained and saved from harm by such bonds; and since each one should keep his body under control by means of such works, there is need that the minister of Christ be far-seeing and faithful. He ought so to govern and teach Christians in all these matters that their conscience and faith will not be offended and that there will not spring up in them a suspicion and a root of bitterness and many will thereby be defiled, as Paul admonishes the Hebrews [Heb. 12:15]; that is, that they may not lose faith and become defiled by the false estimate of the value of works and think that they must be justified by works. Unless faith is at the same time constantly taught, this happens easily and defiles a great many, as has been done until now through the pestilent, impious, soul-destroying traditions of our popes and the opinions of our theologians. By these snares numberless souls have been dragged down to hell, so that you might see in this the work of Antichrist.

In brief, as wealth is the test of poverty, business the test of faithfulness, honors the test of humility, feasts the test of temperance, pleasures the test of chastity, so ceremonies are the test of the righteousness of faith. "Can a man," asks Solomon, "carry fire in his bosom and his clothes and not be burned?" [Prov. 6:27]. Yet as a man must live in the midst of wealth, business, honors, pleasures, and feasts, so also must he live in the midst of cere-monies, that is, in the midst of dangers. Indeed, as infant boys need beyond all else to be cherished in the bosoms and by the hands of maidens to keep them from perishing, yet when they are grown up their salvation is endangered if they asso-ciate with maidens, so the inexperienced and perverse youth need to be restrained and trained by the iron bars of cere-monies lest their unchecked ardor rush headlong into vice after vice. On the other hand, it would be death for them al-ways to be held in bondage to cere-monies, thinking that these justify them. They are rather to be taught that they have been so imprisoned in ceremonies, not that they should be made righteous or gain great merit by them, but that they might thus be kept from doing evil and might more easily be instructed to the righteousness of faith. Such instruction they would not endure if the impulsive-ness of their youth were not restrained.

Hence ceremonies are to be given the same place in the life of a Christian as models and plans have among builders and artisans. They are prepared, not as a permanent structure, but because without them nothing could be built or made. When the structure is complete the models and plans are laid aside. You see, they are not despised, rather they are greatly sought after; but what we despise is the false estimate of them since no one holds them to be the real and permanent structure.

If any man were so flagrantly foolish as to care for nothing all his life long except the most costly, careful, and persistent preparation of plans and models and never to think of the structure itself, and were satisfied with his work in producing such plans and mere aids to work, and boasted of it, would not all men pity his insanity and think that something great might have been built with what he has wasted? Thus we do not despise ceremonies and works, but we set great store by them; but we despise the false estimate placed upon works in order that no one

may think that they are true righteousness, as those hypocrites believe who
spend and lose their whole lives in zeal
for works and never reach that goal for
the sake of which the works are to be
done, who, as the Apostle says, "will listen to anybody and can never arrive at a
knowledge of the truth" [2 Tim. 3:7]. They
seem to wish to build, they make their
preparations, and yet they never build.
Thus they remain caught in the form of
religion and do not attain unto its power
[2 Tim. 3:5]. Meanwhile they are pleased
with their efforts and even dare to judge
all others whom they do not see shining
with a like show of works. Yet with the
gifts of God which they have spent and
abused in vain they might, if they had
been filled with faith, have accomplished
great things to their own salvation and
that of others.

Since human nature and natural reason, as it is called, are by nature supersti-
tious and ready to imagine, when laws
and works are prescribed, that righteousness must be obtained through laws and
works; and further, since they are trained

and confirmed in this opinion by the
practice of all earthly lawgivers, it is impossible that they should of themselves
escape from the slavery of works and
come to a knowledge of the freedom of
faith. Therefore there is need of the
prayer that the Lord may give us and
make us *theodidacti*, that is, those taught
by God [John 6:45], and may himself, as
he has promised, write his law in our
hearts; otherwise there is no hope for us.
If he himself does not teach our hearts
this wisdom hidden in mystery [1 Cor.
2:7], nature can only condemn it and
judge it to be heretical because nature is
offended by it and regards it as foolishness. So we see that it happened in the
old days in the case of the apostles and
prophets, and so godless and blind popes
and their flatterers do to me and to those
who are like me. May God at last be mer-
ciful to them and to us and cause his face
to shine upon us that we may know his
way upon earth [Ps. 67:1–2], his salvation among all nations, God, who is
blessed forever [2 Cor. 11:31]. Amen.

An Open Letter
to Pope Leo X

To Leo X, Pope at Rome, Martin Luther wishes salvation in Christ Jesus our Lord. Amen.

Living among the monsters of this age with whom I am now for the third year waging war, I am compelled occasionally to look up to you, Leo, most blessed father, and to think of you. Indeed, since you are occasionally regarded as the sole cause of my warfare, I cannot help thinking of you. To be sure, the undeserved raging of your godless flatterers against me has compelled me to appeal from your see to a future council, despite the decrees of your predecessors Pius and Julius, who with a foolish tyranny forbade such an

appeal. Nevertheless, I have never alien-
ated myself from Your Blessedness to
such an extent that I should not with all
my heart wish you and your see every
blessing, for which I have besought God
with earnest prayers to the best of my
ability. It is true that I have been so bold
as to despise and look down upon those
who have tried to frighten me with the
majesty of your name and authority.
There is one thing, however, which I cannot ignore and which is the cause of my
writing once more to Your Blessedness. It
has come to my attention that I am ac-
cused of great indiscretion, said to be my
great fault, in which, it is said, I have not
spared even your person.

I freely vow that I have, to my knowledge, spoken only good and honorable
words concerning you whenever I have
thought of you. If I had ever done otherwise, I myself could by no means con-
done it, but should agree entirely with the
judgment that others have formed of me;
and I should do nothing more gladly than
recant such indiscretion and impiety. I
have called you a Daniel in Babylon; and

everyone who reads what I have written knows how zealously I defended your innocence against your defamer Sylvester.[1] Indeed, your reputation and the fame of your blameless life, celebrated as they are throughout the world by the writings of many great men, are too well known and too honorable to be assailed by anyone, no matter how great he is. I am not so foolish as to attack one whom all people praise. As a matter of fact, I have always tried, and will always continue, not to attack even those whom the public dishonors for I take no pleasure in the faults of any man, since I am conscious of the beam in my own eye. I could not, indeed, be the first one to cast a stone at the adulteress [John 8:1–11].

I have, to be sure, sharply attacked ungodly doctrines in general, and I have snapped at my opponents, not because of their bad morals, but because of their ungodliness. Rather than repent this in the least, I have determined to persist in that fervent zeal and to despise the judgment of men, following the example of Christ who in his zeal called his opponents "a brood of vipers," "blind fools," "hypocrites," "children of the devil" [Matt. 23:13, 17, 33; John 8:44]. Paul branded Magus [Elymas, the magician] as the "son of the devil, . . . full of all deceit and villainy" [Acts 13:10], and he calls others "dogs," "deceivers," and "adulterers" [Phil 3:2; 2 Cor. 11:13; 2:17]. If you will allow people with sensitive feelings to judge, they would consider no person more stinging and unrestrained in his denunciations than Paul. Who is more stinging than the prophets? Nowadays, it is true, we are made so sensitive by the raving crowd of flatterers that we cry out that we are stung as soon as we meet with disapproval. When we cannot ward off the truth with any other pretext, we flee from it by ascribing it to a fierce temper, impatience, and immodesty. What is the good of salt if it does not bite? Of what use is the edge of a sword if it does not cut? "Cursed is he who does the work of the Lord deceitfully . . ." [Jer. 48:10].

Therefore, most excellent Leo, I beg you to give me a hearing after I have vindicated myself by this letter, and believe me when I say that I have never thought ill of you personally, that I am the kind of a person who would wish you all good things eternally, and that I have no quarrel with any man concerning his morals but only concerning the word of truth. In all other matters I will yield to any man whatsoever; but I have neither the power nor the will to deny the Word of God. If any man has a different opinion concerning me, he does not think straight or understand what I have actually said.

I have truly despised your see, the Roman Curia, which, however, neither you nor anyone else can deny is more corrupt than any Babylon or Sodom ever was, and which, as far as I can see, is characterized by a completely depraved, hopeless, and notorious godlessness. I have been thoroughly incensed over the fact that good Christians are mocked in your name, and under the cloak of the Roman church I have resisted and will continue to resist your see as long as the spirit of faith lives in me. Not that I shall strive for the impossible or hope that by my efforts alone anything will be accomplished in that most disordered Babylon, where the fury of so many flatterers is turned against me; but I acknowledge my indebtedness to my Christian brethren, whom I am duty-bound to warn so that fewer of them may be destroyed by the plagues of Rome, at least so that their destruction may be less cruel.

As you well know, there has been flowing from Rome these many years—like a flood covering the world—nothing but a devastation of men's bodies and souls and possessions, the worst examples of the worst of all things. All this is clearer than day to all, and the Roman church, once the holiest of all, has become the most licentious den of thieves [Matt. 21:13], the most shameless of all brothels, the kingdom of sin, death, and hell. It is so bad that even Antichrist himself, if he should come, could think of nothing to add to its wickedness.

Meanwhile you, Leo, sit as a lamb in the midst of wolves [Matt. 10:16] and like Daniel in the midst of lions [Dan. 6:16].

With Ezekiel you live among scorpions [Ezek. 2:6]. How can you alone oppose these monsters? Even if you would call to your aid three or four well-learned and thoroughly reliable cardinals, what are these among so many? You would all be poisoned[2] before you could begin to issue a decree for the purpose of remedying the situation. The Roman Curia is already lost, for God's wrath has relentlessly fallen upon it. It detests church councils, it fears a reformation, it cannot allay its own corruption; and what was said of its mother Babylon also applies to it: "We would have cured Babylon, but she was not healed. Let us forsake her" [Jer. 51:9].

It was your duty and that of your cardinals to remedy these evils, but the gout of these evils makes a mockery of the healing hand, and neither chariot nor horse responds to the rein [Virgil, *Georgics* i.514]. Moved by this affection for you, I have always been sorry, most excellent Leo, that you were made pope in these times, for you are worthy of being pope in better days. The Roman Curia does not deserve to have you or men like you, but it should have Satan himself as pope, for he now actually rules in that Babylon more than you do.

Would that you might discard that which your most profligate enemies boastfully claim to be your glory and might live on a small priestly income of your own or on your family inheritance! No persons are worthy of glorying in that honor except the Iscariots, the sons of perdition. What do you accomplish in the Roman Curia, my Leo? The more criminal and detestable a man is, the more gladly will he use your name to destroy men's possessions and souls, to increase crime, to suppress faith and truth and God's whole church. O most unhappy Leo, you are sitting on a most dangerous throne. I am telling you the truth because I wish you well.

If Bernard felt sorry for Eugenius[3] at a time when the Roman See, which, although even then very corrupt, was ruled with better prospects for improvement, why should not we complain who for three hundred years have had such a great increase of corruption and wickedness? Is it not true that under the vast expanse of heaven there is nothing more corrupt, more pestilential, more offensive than the Roman Curia? It surpasses beyond all comparison the godlessness of the Turks so that, indeed, although it was once a gate of heaven, it is now an open mouth of hell, such a mouth that it cannot be shut because of the wrath of God. Only one thing can we try to do, as I have said:[4] we may be able to call back a few from that yawning chasm of Borne and save them.

Now you see, my Father Leo, how and why I have so violently attacked that pestilential see. So far have I been from raving against your person that I even hoped I might gain your favor and save you if I should make a strong and stinging assault upon that prison, that veritable hell of yours. For you and your salvation and the salvation of many others with you will be served by everything that men of ability can do against the confusion of this wicked Curia. They serve your office who do every harm to the Curia; they glorify Christ who in

every way curse it. In short, they are
Christians who are not Romans.

To enlarge upon this, I never intended
to attack the Roman Curia or to raise any
controversy concerning it. But when I
saw all efforts to save it were hopeless, I
despised it, gave it a bill of divorce [Deut.
24:1], and said, "Let the evildoer still do
evil, and the filthy still be filthy" [Rev.
22:11]. Then I turned to the quiet and
peaceful study of the Holy Scriptures so
that I might be helpful to my brothers
around me. When I had made some
progress in these studies, Satan opened
his eyes and then filled his servant Johann Eck, a notable enemy of Christ, with
an insatiable lust for glory and thus
aroused him to drag me unawares to a
debate, seizing me by means of one little
word which I had let slip concerning the
primacy of the Roman church. Then that
boastful braggart,[5] frothing and gnashing
his teeth, declared that he would risk
everything for the glory of God and the
honor of the Apostolic See. Puffed up
with the prospect of abusing your authority, he looked forward with great confi-

dence to a victory over me. He was concerned not so much with establishing the primacy of Peter as he was with demonstrating his own leadership among the theologians of our time. To that end he considered it no small advantage to triumph over Luther. When the debate ended badly for the sophist, an unbelievable madness overcame the man, for he believed that it was his fault alone, which was responsible for my disclosing all the infamy of Rome.

Allow me, I pray, most excellent Leo, this once to plead my cause and to indict your real enemies. You know, I believe, what dealings your legate, cardinal of St. Sisto,[6] an unwise and unfortunate, or rather, an unreliable man, had with me. When out of reverence for your name I had placed myself and my cause in his hands, he did not try to establish peace. He could easily have done so with a single word, for at that time I promised to keep silent and to end the controversy, provided my opponents were ordered to do likewise. As he was a man who sought glory, however, and was not content with such an agreement, he began to defend my opponents, to give them full freedom, and to order me to recant, even though this was not included in his instructions. When matters went fairly well, he with his churlish arbitrariness made them far worse. Therefore Luther is not to blame for what followed. All the blame is Cajetan's, who did not permit me to keep silent, as I at that time most earnestly requested him to do. What more should I have done?

There followed Karl Miltitz,[7] also a nuncio of Your Holiness, who exerted much effort and traveled back and forth, omitting nothing that might help restore the order which Cajetan had rashly and arrogantly disturbed. He finally, with the help of the most illustrious prince, the Elector Frederick, managed to arrange several private conferences with me.[8] Again I yielded out of respect for your name, was prepared to keep silent, and even accepted as arbiter either the archbishop of Trier or the bishop of Naumburg. So matters were arranged. But while this arrangement was being followed with good prospects of success, behold, that other and greater enemy of yours, Eck, broke in with the Leipzig Debate which he had undertaken against Dr. Karlstadt. When the new question of the primacy of the pope was raised, he suddenly turned his weapons against me and completely upset our arrangement for maintaining peace. Meanwhile Karl Miltitz waited. The debate was held and judges were selected. But again no decision was reached, which is not surprising, for through Eck's lies, tricks, and wiles everything was stirred up, aggravated, and confused worse than ever. Regardless of the decision, which might have been reached, a greater conflagration would have resulted, for he sought glory, not the truth. Again I left undone nothing that I ought to have done.

I admit that on this occasion no small amount of corrupt Roman practices came to light, but whatever wrong was done was Eck's fault, who undertook a task beyond his capacities. Striving insanely for his own glory, he revealed the shame of Rome to all the world. This man is your enemy, my dear Leo, or rather the enemy of your Curia. From his example alone we can learn that no enemy is more pernicious than a flatterer. What did he accomplish with his flattery but an evil, which not even a king could have accomplished? The name of the Roman Curia is today a stench throughout the world, papal authority languishes, and Roman ignorance, once honored, is in ill repute. We should have heard nothing of all this if Eck had not upset the peace arrangements made by Karl [von Miltitz] and myself. Eck himself now clearly sees this and, although it is too late and to no avail, he is furious that my books were published. He should have thought of this when, like a whinnying horse, he was madly seeking his own glory and preferred his own advantage through you and at the greatest peril to you. The vain man thought that I would stop and keep silent out of fear for your name, for I do not believe that he entirely trusted his cleverness and learning. Now that he sees that I have more courage than that and have not been silenced, he repents of his rashness, but too late, and perceives—if indeed he does finally understand—that there is One in heaven who opposes the proud and humbles the haughty [1 Pet. 5:5; Jth. 6:15].

Since we gained nothing from this debate except greater confusion to the Roman cause, Karl Miltitz, in a third attempt to bring about peace, came to the fathers of the Augustinian Order assembled in their chapter and sought their advice in settling the controversy which had now grown most disturbing and dangerous. Because, by God's favor, they had no hope of proceeding against me by violent means, some of their most famous men were sent to me. These men asked me at least to show honor to the person of Your Blessedness and in a humble letter to plead as my excuse your innocence and mine in the matter. They said that the affair was not yet in a hopeless state, provided Leo X out of his innate goodness would take a hand in it. As I have always both offered and desired peace so that I might devote myself to quieter and more useful studies, and have stormed with such great fury merely for the purpose of overwhelming my unequal opponents by the volume and violence of words no less than of intellect, I not only gladly ceased but also joyfully and thankfully considered this suggestion a very welcome kindness to me, provided our hope could be realized.

So I come, most blessed father, and, prostrate before you, pray that if possible you intervene and stop those flatterers, who are the enemies of peace while they pretend to keep peace. But let no person imagine that I will recant unless he prefer to involve the whole question in even greater turmoil. Furthermore, I acknowledge no fixed rules for the interpretation of the Word of God, since the Word of God, which teaches freedom in all other matters, must not be bound [2 Tim. 2:9]. If these two points are granted, there is nothing that I could not or would not most willingly do or endure. I detest contentions. I will challenge no one. On the other hand, I do not want others to challenge me. If they do, as Christ is my teacher, I will not be speechless. When once this controversy has been cited before you and settled, Your Blessedness will be able with a brief and ready word to silence both parties and command them to keep the peace. That is what I have always wished to hear.

Therefore, my Father Leo, do not listen to those sirens who pretend that you are no mere man but a demigod so that you may command and require whatever you wish. It will not be done in that manner and you will not have such remarkable power. You are a servant of servants,[9] and more than all other men you are in a most miserable and dangerous position. Be not deceived by those who pretend that you are lord of the world, allow no one to be considered a Christian unless he accepts your authority, and boast that you have power over heaven, hell, and purgatory. These men are your enemies who seek to destroy your soul [1 Kings 19:10], as Isaiah says: "O my people, they that call thee blessed, the same deceive thee" [Isa. 3:12]. They err who exalt you above a council and the church universal. They err who ascribe to you alone the right of interpreting Scripture. Under the protection of your name they seek to gain support for all their wicked deeds in the church. Alas! Through them Satan has already made much progress under your predecessors. In short, believe none who exalt you, believe those who humble you. This is the judgment of God, that "he has put down the mighty from their thrones and exalted those of low degree" [Luke 1:52]. See how different Christ is from his successors, although they all would wish to be his vicars. I fear that most of them have been too literally his vicars. A man is a vicar only when his superior is absent. If the pope rules, while Christ is absent and does not dwell in his heart, what else is he but a vicar of Christ? What is the church under such a vicar but a mass of people without Christ? Indeed, what is such a vicar but an antichrist and an idol? How much more properly did the apostles call themselves servants of the present Christ and not vicars of an absent Christ?

Perhaps I am presumptuous in trying to instruct so exalted a personage from whom we all should learn and from whom the thrones of judges receive their decisions, as those pestilential fellows of yours boast. But I am following the example of St. Bernard in his book, *On Consideration,*[10] to Pope Eugenius, a book every pope should know from memory. I follow him, not because I am eager to instruct you, but out of pure and loyal concern which compels us to be interested in all the affairs of our neighbors, even when they are protected, and which does not permit us to take into consideration either their dignity or lack of dignity since it is only concerned with the dangers they face or the advantages they may gain. I know that Your Blessedness is driven and buffeted about in home, that is, that far out at sea you are threatened on all sides by dangers and are working very hard in the miserable situation so that you are in need of even the slightest help of the least of your brothers. Therefore I do not consider it absurd if I now forget your exalted office and do what brotherly love demands. I have no desire to flatter you in so serious and dangerous a matter. If men do not perceive that I am your friend and your most humble subject in this matter, there is One who understands and judges [John 8:50].

Finally, that I may not approach you empty-handed, blessed father, I am sending you this little treatise dedicated to you as a token of peace and good hope.[11] From this book you may judge with what studies I should prefer to be more profitably occupied, as I could be, provided your godless flatterers would permit me and had permitted me in the past. It is a small book if you regard its size. Unless I am mistaken, however, it contains the whole of Christian life in a brief form, provided you grasp its meaning. I am a poor man and have no other gift to offer, and you do not need to be enriched by any but a spiritual gift. May the Lord Jesus preserve you forever. Amen.

Wittenberg
September 6, 1520

Notes

1. Sylvester Mazzolini (1456–1523), usually
    called Prierias after Prierio, the city of his
    birth, had published three books against
    Luther. In these he had exaggerated the au-
    thority of the papacy.
2. An attempt to poison Leo X had been made
    the summer of 1517.
3. Bernard of Clairvaux wrote a devotional book,
    On Consideration, to Pope Eugenius III
    (1145–53), in which he discussed the duties of
    the pope and the dangers connected with his
    office. J.-P. Migne, *Patrilogia Latina*, vol. 182:
    727–808.
4. Cf. p. 51, par. 1 above.
5. Thraso, in the original Latin, is the name of a
    braggart soldier in Terence's *Eunuch*.

6. Cardinal Thomas Cajetan. Jacopo de Vio Gaeta assumed the names Thomas in honor of St. Thomas of Aquinas and Cajetan, derived from Gaeta, the place of his origin.

7. Karl von Miltitz had induced Luther to be silent with respect to the indulgence controversy, provided his opponents did likewise.

8. At Altenburg on January 5 or 6, 1519.

9. *Servus servorum* [servant of servants] was the usual title of the Pope.

10. Cf. n. 3 above.

11. *On Christian Liberty* [*The Freedom of a Christian*].